W9-BYQ-788

ARGENTINA

Big Buddy Books

An Imprint of Abdo Publishing
www.abdopublishing.com

Julie Murray

www.abdopublishing.com

Published by Abdo Publishing, a division of ABDO, PO Box 398166, Minneapolis, Minnesota 55439.
Copyright © 2015 by Abdo Consulting Group, Inc. International copyrights reserved in all countries. No part
of this book may be reproduced in any form without written permission from the publisher. Big Buddy Books™
is a trademark and logo of Abdo Publishing.

Printed in the United States of America, North Mankato, Minnesota.
032014
092014

THIS BOOK CONTAINS
RECYCLED MATERIALS

Cover Photo: Shutterstock.
Interior Photos: ASSOCIATED PRESS (pp. 15, 16, 17, 19, 31, 33, 35), iStockphoto (pp. 11, 21, 23, 25, 35),
    Shutterstock (pp. 5, 9, 13, 19, 27, 29, 34, 37, 38).

Coordinating Series Editor: Rochelle Baltzer
Editor: Sarah Tieck
Contributing Editors: Bridget O'Brien, Marcia Zappa
Graphic Design: Adam Craven

Country population and area figures taken from the CIA World Factbook.

Library of Congress Cataloging-in-Publication Data

Murray, Julie, 1969-
  Argentina / Julie Murray.
      pages cm. -- (Explore the countries)
  ISBN 978-1-62403-341-4
1. Argentina--Juvenile literature. I. Title.
F2808.2.M87 2014
982--dc23
                                    2013051237

ARGENTINA

CONTENTS

AROUND THE WORLD

Our world has many countries. Each country has beautiful land. It has its own rich history. And, the people have their own languages and ways of life.

Argentina is a country in South America. What do you know about Argentina? Let's learn more about this place and its story!

Did You Know?

Argentina's official language is Spanish.

Iguazú Falls is known for its grand beauty. These waterfalls are on the border between Argentina and Brazil.

Passport to Argentina

Argentina is in southern South America. It borders five countries and an ocean.

Argentina's total area is 1,073,518 square miles (2,780,400 sq km). More than 43 million people live there.

WHERE IN THE WORLD?

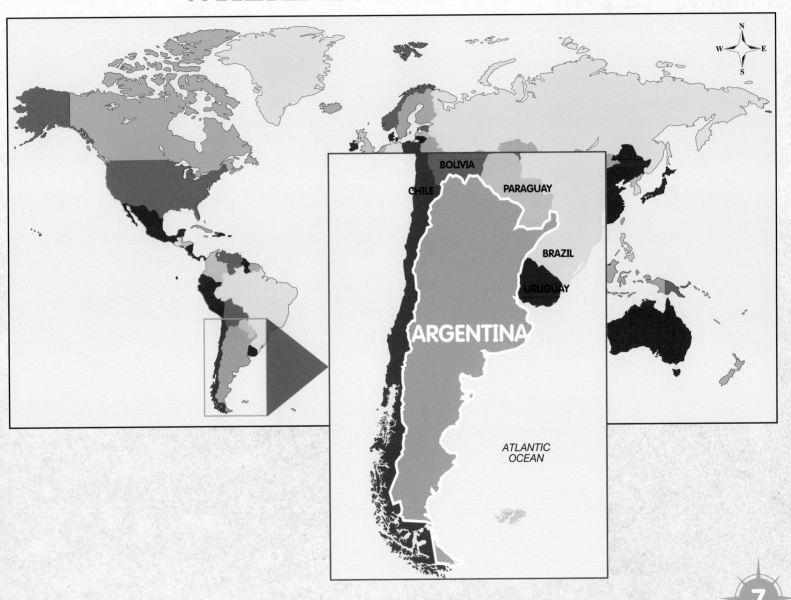

IMPORTANT CITIES

Buenos Aires is Argentina's capital and largest city. It has about 2.8 million people. Many more live in the cities and towns around it. The city is located on a bay. It is the country's main port.

Buenos Aires is a center for business. It has factories, universities, museums, and government offices.

SAY IT

Buenos Aires
bway-nuhs A-reez

Did You Know?

Buenos Aires means "fair winds" in Spanish.

The Pink House is located in Buenos Aires. It is where the president works.

Córdoba

Rosario

Buenos Aires

ARGENTINA

N
W E
S

Córdoba is Argentina's second-largest city. About 1.3 million people live there. The city is on the Primero River and near the Cordoba Mountains. Cars, tractors, cloth, and glass are made there.

Rosario is the country's third-largest city. It is home to more than 908,000 people. The city is on the Paraná River in the Pampas. This area is known for farming.

SAY IT

Córdoba
KAWR-duh-buh

Rosario
roh-ZAHR-ee-oh

Córdoba was founded in 1573.

Rosario is an important port and a center for business.

11

Argentina in History

The first people to live in what is now Argentina were native tribes. Some hunted and fished. Others farmed crops, including corn.

Europeans arrived in the 1500s. In 1516, Juan Díaz de Solís claimed land for Spain. But, he and others were killed by the natives. In 1580, the Spanish made a lasting settlement at Buenos Aires. Over time, they ruled the area.

San Ignacio Mini opened in the 1600s to teach tribes about Christianity. Today, people can see the remains of the buildings.

The people of Argentina did not like being ruled by Spain. In 1816, they declared independence. At first, they didn't agree on how to run the country.

By the 1880s, the country had **united** and began to grow. One important business was **exporting** meat and grains to Europe. This made Argentina one of the world's richest countries by the 1920s.

Starting in 1930, Argentina was led off and on by military leaders. The country struggled. Today, it is led by a president.

In 1946, Juan Perón was chosen as president. He helped city workers, but he also took away people's freedoms.

15

TIMELINE

1903

Buenos Aires police started using Juan Vucetich's way of using fingerprints to solve crimes. His system is still used in some countries.

1853

Argentina adopted a constitution.

1944

Jorge Luis Borges of Buenos Aires printed *Ficciones*. It was one of his most famous works.

1986

Star player Diego Maradona led the country's soccer team to win the World Cup. Maradona was known for scoring points.

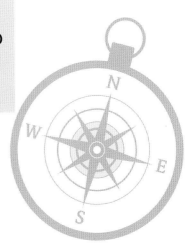

2013

On March 13, Cardinal Jorge Bergoglio of Argentina was chosen as pope. He took the name Pope Francis.

1954

Pascual Perez became the country's first World Boxing Champion.

An Important Symbol

Argentina's flag has three stripes. Two are blue and one is white. In the center of the white stripe is a sun. This design came into use in 1818.

Argentina's government is a **federal republic**. Groups called the Senate and the Chamber of Deputies make laws. The president is the head of state and government.

The sun on Argentina's flag stands for freedom from Spain.

In 2007, Cristina Fernández de Kirchner became president.

ACROSS THE LAND

Argentina has mountains, grasslands, and **plateaus**. The Andes Mountains run down the country's western border.

The Pampas is a grassy plain in the heart of the country. Patagonia is a plateau south of the Pampas.

The Pampas has some of the world's richest soil.

Did You Know?

When it is winter in North America, it is summer in Argentina. In January, northern Argentina's average temperature is about 80°F (27°C). In July, it is about 60°F (16°C).

Argentina's animals include monkeys, llamas, and capybaras. Whales and sea lions live in the coastal waters. Penguins live near the country's coasts.

A wide variety of plants grow on the land. There are holly trees, fruit trees, and grape plants. Some flat and mountain areas have hardly any trees.

The capybara is the world's largest rodent! It can be up to 145 pounds (66 kg)!

Earning a Living

In Argentina, most people work in service jobs. They may work for the government or help visitors to the country. Others work in factories that make cars, cloth, or food.

Argentina has important natural resources. Farmers grow corn, soybeans, wheat, and fruit. The country is a leading producer of beef. Shrimp, scallops, and squid come from its waters.

Argentina is a world leader in growing corn, soybeans, and wool.

Life in Argentina

Most of Argentina's people live in cities. They often live in apartments. Others live in the countryside in houses or huts.

The people of Argentina enjoy eating meat. They often cook it over a grill or open fire. Favorite cookies or desserts often include a milky caramel. People drink maté tea and wine.

Caminito is a street in Buenos Aires known for its bright buildings.

Did You Know?

In Argentina, children must attend school from ages 5 to 14.

27

Soccer, or football, is Argentina's most popular sport. People also play basketball and rugby. Car and horse racing are popular as well.

Most of the country's people are Roman Catholic. There are beautiful churches throughout the country.

Basílica de Nuestra Señora del Pilar was built in 1732. This church is located in Buenos Aires.

FAMOUS FACES

Eva Duarte de Perón was born on May 7, 1919, near Buenos Aires. Her given name was María Eva Duarte. She was a popular and powerful First Lady.

Eva was an actress when she married Juan Perón in 1945. The next year, he became the country's president. Eva supported the rights of workers and women. She died on July 26, 1952, after fighting an illness.

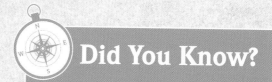

Did You Know?

Eva Perón was also known as Evita. The musical *Evita* was written about her life.

Eva wanted to become Argentina's vice president. But, the army stopped her from running because she was a woman.

People were interested in Eva's style.

Pope Francis was born on December 17, 1936, in Buenos Aires. His given name was Jorge Mario Bergoglio.

Pope Francis was chosen as pope in 2013. He was the first pope from Latin America. As pope, he is the leader of the Roman Catholic Church. He is known for helping the poor and for his simple way of life.

Pope Francis often visits churches and meets people.

Tour Book

Imagine traveling to Argentina! Here are some places you could go and things you could do.

 **Explore**

Visit the city of Ushuaia. It is one of the southernmost cities in the world. People travel there to ski, see whales and penguins, and get close to Antarctica.

 See

Bariloche is a town near the Andes Mountains. People stroll the charming streets. They also visit the area's mountains and lakes.

 ## Play

Join a soccer game! People often play in parks. And, Argentina is home to world-famous soccer players. So if you don't find a game to join, you can watch one on television.

 ## Do

See a parade of cowboys on Tradition Day in San Antonia de Areco. This event has been held for about 75 years. It includes music, dancing, and food.

 ## Dance

Argentina is famous for a dance called the tango. It started in Buenos Aires. Over time, it became the country's national dance and music.

A Great Country

The story of Argentina is important to our world. Argentina is a land of beautiful waterfalls and mountains. It is a country of strong people with new ideas.

The people and places that make up Argentina offer something special. They help make the world a more interesting place.

The Andes Mountains go all the way to Argentina's tip. They stretch north through several countries.

Argentina Up Close

Official Name: República Argentina (Argentine Republic)

Flag:

Population (rank): 43,024,374 (July 2014 est.) (33rd most-populated country)

Total Area (rank): 1,073,518 square miles (8th largest country)

Capital: Buenos Aires

Official Language: Spanish

Currency: Argentine peso

Form of Government: Federal republic

National Anthem: "Himno Nacional Argentino" (Argentine National Anthem)

IMPORTANT WORDS

capital a city where government leaders meet.

Catholic of or relating to the Roman Catholic Church. This kind of Christianity has been around since the first century and is led by the pope.

constitution the basic laws that govern a country or a state.

export to send goods to another country for sale.

federal republic a form of government in which the people choose the leader. The central government and the individual states share power.

natural resources useful and valued supplies from nature.

plateau (pla-TOH) a raised area of flat land.

unite (yu-NITE) to come together for a purpose or action.

WEBSITES

To learn more about Explore the Countries, visit **booklinks.abdopublishing.com**. These links are routinely monitored and updated to provide the most current information available.

INDEX